Praise for

The Princes of Serendip

"This delightful story will be appreciated by children as well as the adults in their lives. Children are likely to be engaged by the premise, settings, and patterns within the book. Adults will welcome the opportunity to help instill in children values including pride in work, gratitude, and kindness. Congratulations to Allyson Apsey for this impressive debut in picture book writing."

—Nell K. Duke, professor of literacy, language, and culture, University of Michigan

"Picture books are one of my favorite things to share with children. But more than just a good picture book, I always want to share one that has a story that will resonate with the child. Allyson Apsey has created a sweet story about three princes and the lessons they learn about kindness, gratitude, and pride—lessons that are so important for every child to hear."

—Todd Nesloney, award-winning educator and bestselling author

"Allyson's words weave a story of compassion and kindness and share ways in which we can build a little empathy into each of our days. *The Princes of Serendip* is a must-read for all learners and ages."

—Jessica Cabeen, National Distinguished Principal, author of *Hacking Early Learning* and coauthor of *Balance Like a Pirate*

"As a parent and educator, I love how Allyson encapsulates three beautiful important messages into one book. I was drawn into the story as I read how each prince shared their real-world experiences of life in someone else's shoes and reflected on their experience with family. *The Princes of Serendip* provides us true examples of warmth, empathy, kindness, and ways in which we can be proud of who we are and what we do. And my daughters *love* this book! They loved how the princes learned kindness, love, and gratitude. My oldest daughter said, 'The story made me feel great because the princes were working hard to help people in need. I love how they saw the beauty in others.'"

—Karen Festa, wife, mom, and passionate educator

The Princes of Serendip

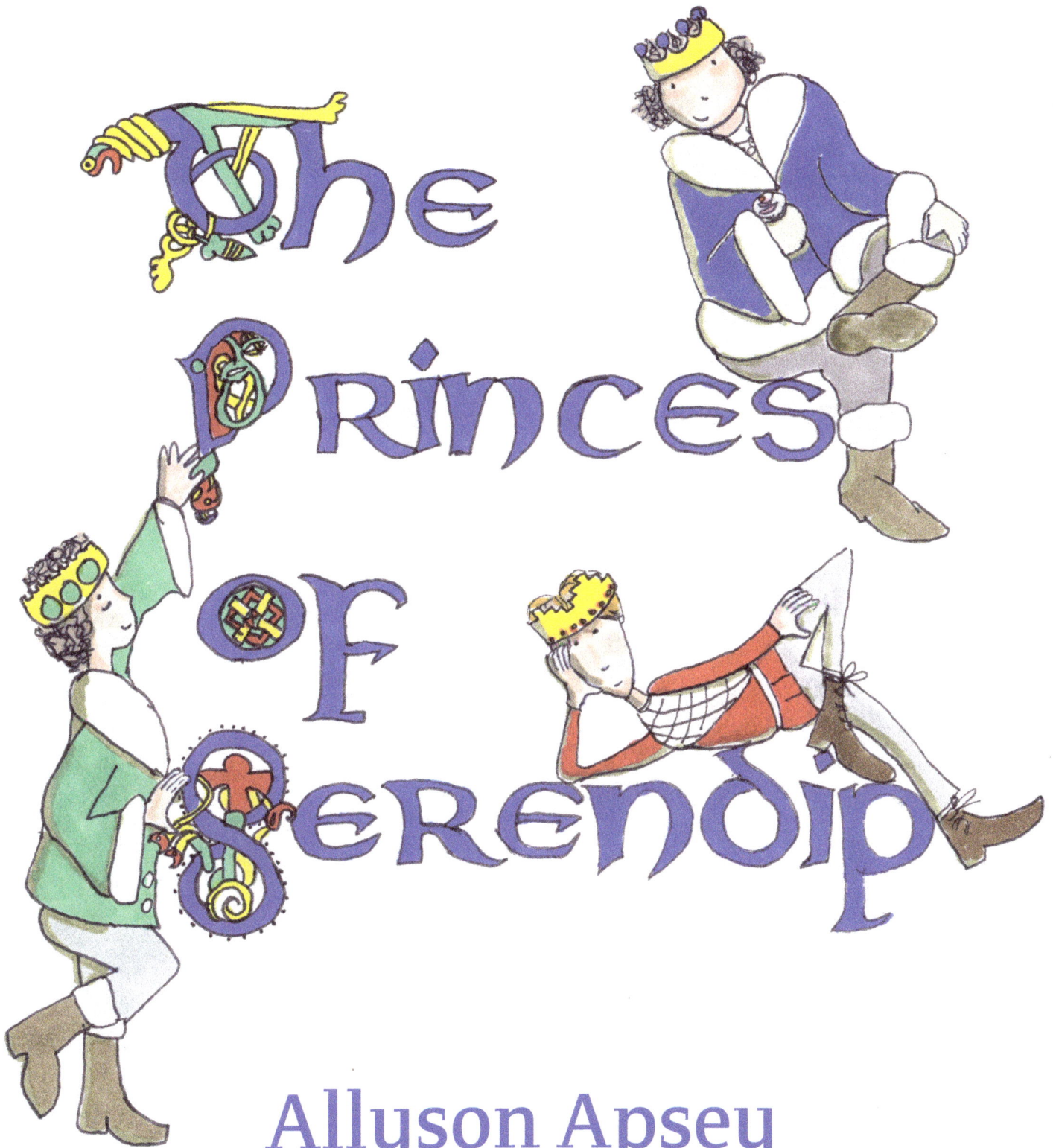

Allyson Apsey

Illustrated by Molly Blaisdell

This book is available at special discounts when purchased in quantity for use as premiums, promotions, fundraisers, or for educational use. For inquiries and details, contact the publisher at books@daveburgessconsulting.com.

For more books from Dave Burgess Consulting, Inc., visit DaveBurgessConsulting.com/dbcibooks.

Published by Dave Burgess Consulting, Inc.
San Diego, CA
DaveBurgessConsulting.com

Cover Design and Illustrations by *Molly Blaisdell*
Editing and Interior Design by My Writers' Connection

Paperback ISBN: 978-1-949595-01-7
Hardcover: 978-1-949595-02-4
LCCN: 2018961081

First Printing: November 2018

DEDICATION

This book is dedicated to the students, staff, and families of Quincy Elementary in Zeeland, Michigan. You inspire me to learn, grow, and find joy in every day, and I am so grateful for you.

There once were three princes who lived in a village called Serendip.

They lounged and napped in their castle and ate to their hearts' content.

They polished their jeweled crowns
and ordered servants around.

All in all, they thought life was
pretty grand.

Then one day when their father, the king of Serendip, visited them, he asked, "What will you do when you grow up? Who will you be?"

They looked to each other and then to their father and said, "We like our life just the way it is."

"We like ordering our servants around, eating delicacies, wearing lavish clothing, and napping the day away."

"Why, oh why would we want to do anything else?"

The king hung his head and sighed a deep sigh. "My sons, I have spoiled you. All hope is lost for this kingdom."

He solemnly walked out of the castle shaking his head. The princes saw a tear escape his eye.

"Oh, no!" said the three princes of Serendip, for they loved their father very much, and it hurt their hearts to see him so disappointed.

"Are we spoiled?" asked one.

"What should we do?" asked another.

"We need to make our father proud," said the third.

Instead of napping that afternoon, they took a walk into the village. As they watched the villagers go about their daily business, one of the brothers had an idea.

"I know!" he said. "We should spend a week living as common villagers. We could see all the jobs they do, and that could help us decide what we would like to do when we grow up."

Another brother replied, "But that sounds like so much work!"

The third brother whined, "And who would feed us and dress us?"

"Brothers! You saw how disappointed our father was. It is time we grow up and start doing things for ourselves."

His brothers could not think of any other arguments, so they decided to go along with the plan.

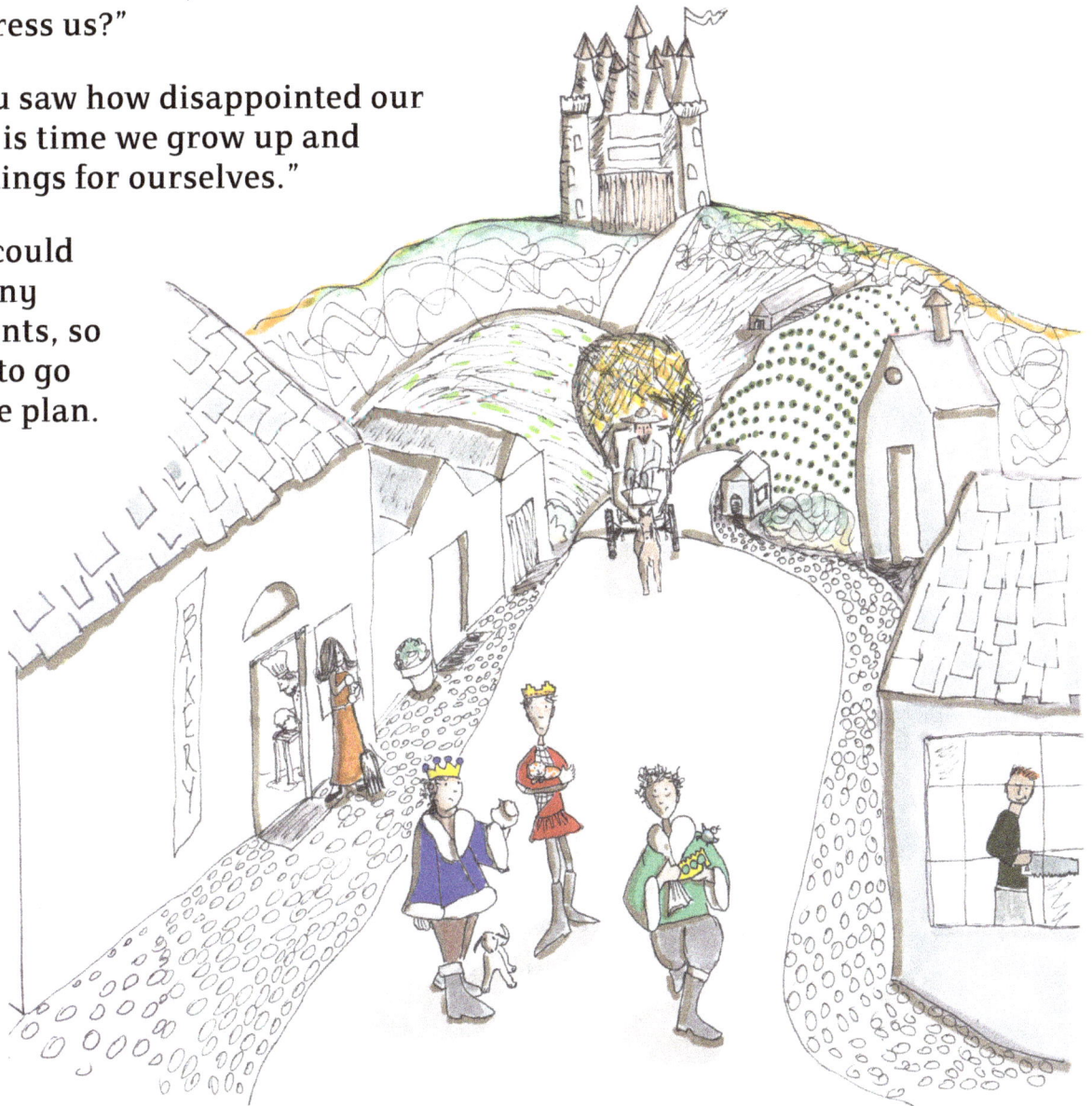

They went home and packed up a few of their things, and they ventured off in different directions, each prince looking for a villager to take him in for a week.

The first brother found a farmer with a little family and a bountiful crop. The farmer put the prince to work right away tending to the harvest, feeding the animals, and preparing food for dinner.

Later that night, as the prince settled into the pile of hay that was to be his bed, his muscles ached, and his hands were starting to callus.

This is no life for a prince, he thought just before he fell into a deep sleep.

He woke in the morning to hear the farmer whistling as he worked while his son ran alongside him, saying, "Father, look at this! Father, look at that!"

The farmer's wife called out to the prince, "Good morning, Your Royal Highness! Please join us for breakfast."

The prince saw such joy on the family members' faces, and he wondered, *How could they love this life of hard labor and little rest?*

At the table, the farmer's wife proudly presented breakfast to the prince. "We grow the most delicious corn, and our hens lay the largest eggs in the village. My husband and son work so beautifully side by side. Our life is a blessed one."

As the prince thought about all he had accomplished the day before on the farm, he felt something warm in his heart—an emotion he didn't recognize—for he had never felt proud of himself before. He realized then that taking *pride* in his work is one of life's purest joys.

The village carpenter welcomed the second brother but not before warning the young man that he expected him to work hard. He had an important project to finish.

They approached an old cottage with worn-out wood planks and a chimney that looked more like a crooked hat.

"However will we repair this cottage?" asked the prince as he surveyed the run-down home.

"And if we do, how will this poor villager pay you?"

The carpenter handed the prince a hammer, and he paused before he answered. "This villager is an old woman who spent her life caring for the poor, never worrying about being paid. The least we can do is repair her cottage to give her a comfortable place to spend the rest of her days."

The carpenter and the prince worked until the sun set.

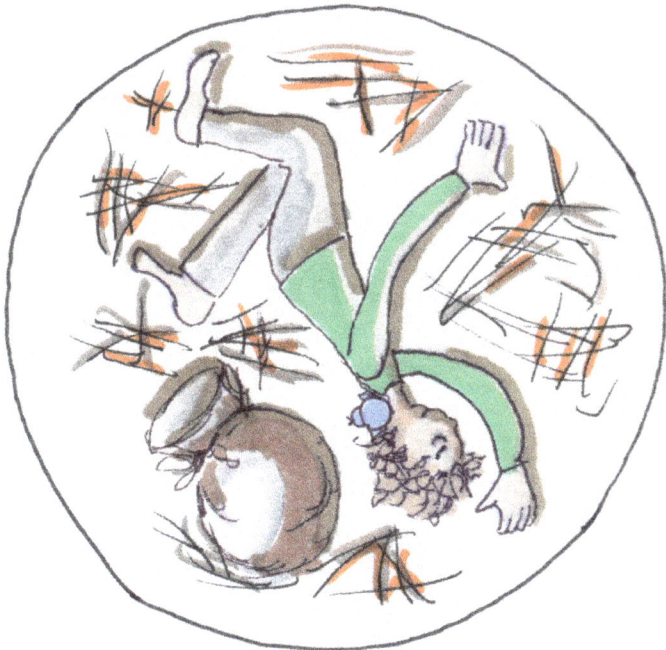

Later that night, as the prince settled into the pile of hay that was to be his bed, his muscles ached, and his hands were starting to callus.

This is no life for a prince, he thought just before he fell into a deep sleep.

When the carpenter and the prince arrived at the cottage the next day, the old woman greeted them at the door.

Tears filled her eyes. She kissed the prince's hands as she said, "You have made my cottage a home again. How can I ever repay you?"

The carpenter smiled a big smile, hugged her gently, and said, "You never asked a single person to pay you for your healing work. We are simply giving back a small portion of your kindness."

The prince felt something warm in his heart—an emotion he didn't recognize—for he had never witnessed such kindness before. He realized then that sharing **kindness** is one of life's purest joys.

The third prince spent the week with the village baker. As the baker showed him around the bakery, in walked the baker's daughter. She was a beautiful girl, and her pretty hair covered half of her face.

"She must be shy," thought the prince, and he gave her a big smile. But the girl barely glanced at him as she tied on an apron.

All day long, the prince worked alongside the girl, kneading the dough and preparing it for the oven. All day long, the girl ignored the handsome prince despite his best efforts to entertain her.

As the baker and the prince walked home together that evening, they talked about the day's work. "Your daughter seems very quiet. Is she always like that? I hope I didn't do something to scare her."

"Oh, my prince," said the baker. "My daughter is quiet with everyone."

Later that night, as the prince settled into the pile of hay that was to be his bed, his muscles ached, and his hands were starting to callus.

This is no life for a prince, he thought just before he fell into a deep sleep.

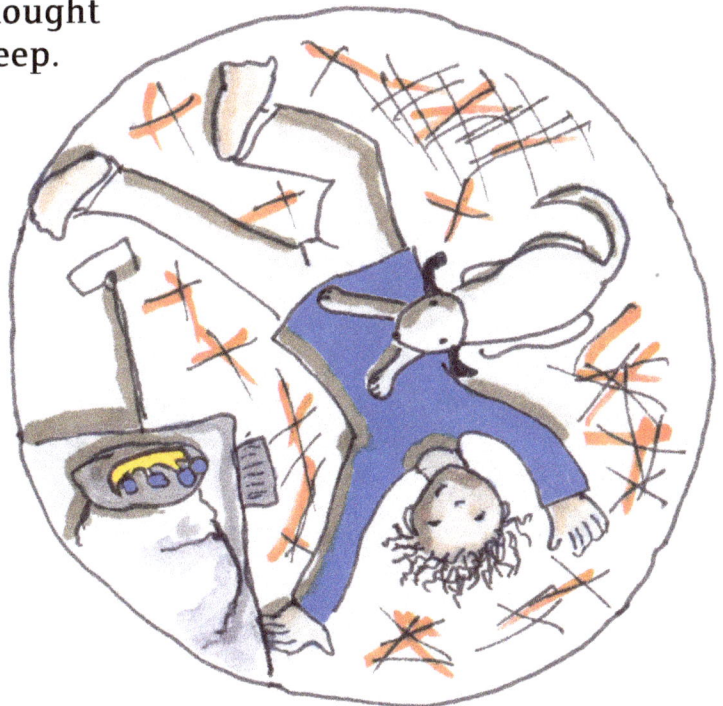

In the morning, the prince walked back to the bakery with the baker. The baker's daughter walked quietly a few paces ahead of them.

Suddenly she turned to watch a deer run into the woods, and for just a moment, the prince saw her face. His breath caught in his chest when he saw the scars that hid beneath her long hair.

Noticing the prince's surprise, the baker gently said, "I am thankful for each one of those scars. Every one represents what I could have lost. My daughter was burned in an accident at our bakery when she was just a wee girl. We thought we had lost her forever, but her injuries miraculously healed. They are a beautiful reminder of how precious and fleeting great love can be. I am eternally grateful that my daughter lives."

The prince felt something warm in his heart—an emotion
he didn't recognize—for he had never felt grateful before.
He realized then that **gratitude** is one of life's purest joys.

After the week spent apart, the princes were very glad to see each other.

They each joyfully exclaimed at the same time, "Brothers! You will not believe what I discovered!"

"Pride!"

"Kindness!"

"Gratitude!"

They seemed to finish each other's sentences as they each agreed, "The villagers live lives filled with hard work and hazards, but there is such beauty in the sweet rewards of their labors!"

Their father overheard their conversation and exclaimed, "My sons! My sons! You have made me so proud. You have discovered the secret of Serendip! The most beautiful lessons are found as we work and love and live each day. That is *serendipity*: the fortunes, the lessons, the joys, and even the sorrows we stumble upon in everything we experience."

"Serendipity! Father, that is it! It is beautiful; we saw it ourselves!" The princes shared their tales of pride, kindness, and gratitude with their father.

This time, his eyes
gleamed with tears
not of sorrow or fear,
but of joy and hope.

The princes never again spent their days lounging and napping or polishing their jeweled crowns. And they stopped ordering their servants around.

Instead, they joined the villagers and worked hard every day.

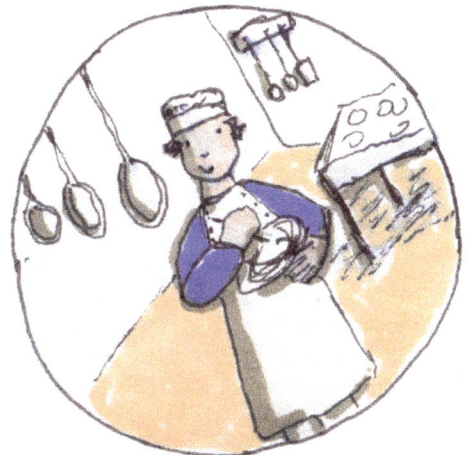

Their muscles ached, and their hands grew more callused. And every night as they lay down to sleep, they counted their blessings and thought,

This is the life for a prince!

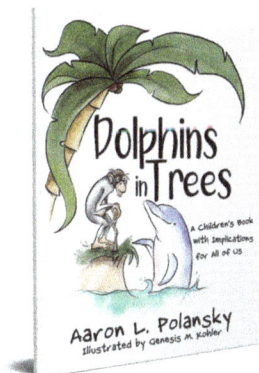

Dolphins in Trees

A Children's Book with Implications for All of Us

by Aaron Polansky

This beautifully illustrated story about kindness and helping others is a must-read in the genre of social-emotional learning. Written for children, it provides incredible jumping-off points for meaningful discussion with readers of all ages. Author and educator Aaron Polansky speaks with students and educators across the country sharing the message: *Love who you are. Love what you do. Help others do the same.*

DaveBurgessConsulting.com/books/dolphins-in-trees

WITH GRATITUDE

I am blessed beyond measure. I have the best job in the world; I work with the most passionate and dedicated educators I have ever met. I have two beautiful sons, a loving husband, and an extended family and dear friends who know the best and the worst of me but love me anyway.

Thank you so much, Dave and Shelley Burgess, for believing in me and for taking a risk on me and for allowing me to share this story. Thank you so much to Erin Casey and team, for taking my manuscript and turning it into this gorgeous book. Finally, a huge thank you to Molly Blaisdell for creating the whimsical, sweet, and beautiful illustrations that bring *The Princes of Serendip* to life.

Love, Allyson

As we express our gratitude, we must never forget that the highest appreciation is not to utter words, but to live by them.

—John F. Kennedy

ABOUT THE AUTHOR

Allyson Apsey loves working with students, staff, and families every day as the principal of Quincy Elementary in Zeeland, Michigan. Her staff and students have been instrumental in making *The Princes of Serendip* come to life, and it has been such a gift to share the writing process with them. Allyson is also the author of *The Path to Serendipity: Discover the Gifts Along Life's Journey*, and she writes on a blog called *Serendipity in Education*, which can be found at AllysonApsey.com.

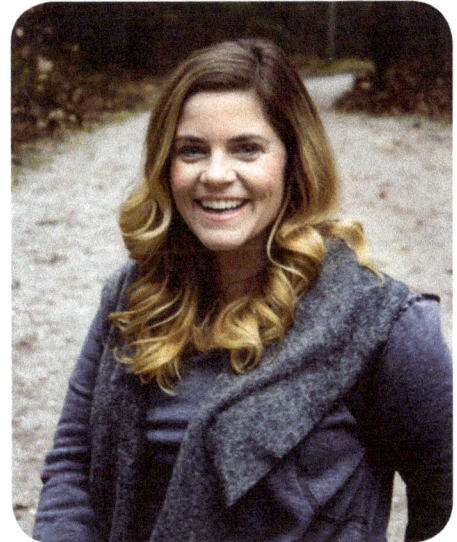

Allyson is honored to serve on the Executive Board of Directors for MEMSPA (Michigan Elementary and Middle School Principals Association). Additionally, she is on the Steering Committee for MACUL (Michigan Association for Computer Users in Learning) SIG-ADMIN. She so enjoys working with and learning from amazing educational leaders in both of these organizations.

Recognizing the significant impact trauma has had on many of our students, staff, and families, Allyson completed a program to become a Certified Trauma Practitioner in Education. She strongly believes that the supports that students affected by trauma need are beneficial to all students because they are grounded in a foundational core of strong, positive relationships based on trust.

Allyson loves speaking to passionate groups of educators as everyone works to be happy and effective people for the benefit of everyone.

Allyson is married to Jim, and they have two amazing sons, Laine and Tyson.

www.ingramcontent.com/pod-product-compliance
Lightning Source LLC
LaVergne TN
LVHW070058080426
835512LV00026B/3490